OCT - - 2009

Pug
What a Mug!

by Lori Haskins Houran

Consultant: Seattle Pug Rescue
Seattle, Washington

PUBLISHING

New York, New York

Credits

Cover and Title Page, © Digital Vision Ltd./Superstock; TOC, © Jesse Kunerth/ Shutterstock; 4, © Bill Ryerson/Winchester Hospital; 5, © Bill Ryerson/Winchester Hospital; 6L, © Kimbell Art Museum, Fort Worth, Texas / Art Resource, NY; 6R, © Pierre Colombel/Corbis; 7, © AP Images/Lucy Pemoni; 8, © William I (1533-84) 'The Silent', Prince of Orange (colour engraving), Hogenberg, Franz (1540-c.1590)/ Bibliotheque Nationale, Paris, France, Archives Charmet/The Bridgeman Art Library; 9, © Condé Nast Archive/Corbis; 10L, © Animal Fair Media/Getty Images; 10R, © Frederick M. Brown/Getty Images; 11T, © Paulette Johnson; 11B, © Jill N. hamilton-Krawczyk / www.pugrescuenetwork.com; 12, © Mark McQueen/ kimballstock; 13, © LWA-Dann Tardif/Corbis; 14, © Corbis/SuperStock; 15L, © Mark Raycroft/Minden Pictures; 15R, © Paulette Johnson; 16L, © Digital Vision Ltd./SuperStock; 16R, © Huntstock, Inc/Alamy; 17, © Paulette Johnson; 18, © Connie Summers/Paulette Johnson; 19, © Jerry Shulman; 20, © Paulette Johnson; 21, © Juniors Bildarchiv/Alamy; 22, © Pets by Paulette; 23, © Lucas Jackson/Reuters/Landov; 24, © Seth Wenig/Reuters/Landov; 25, Westminster Kennel Club Photo; 26, © Volney B Powell/Powell-Ful Creations; 27, © Volney B Powell/Powell-Ful Creations; 28, © Utekhina Anna/Shutterstock; 29, © Creatas/Photolibrary; 31, © Mariusz Szachowski/Shutterstock; 32, © Utekhina Anna/Shutterstock.

Publisher: Kenn Goin
Senior Editor: Lisa Wiseman
Creative Director: Spencer Brinker
Photo Researcher: Amy Dunleavy
Design: Dawn Beard Creative

Library of Congress Cataloging-in-Publication Data

Haskins, Lori
 Pug : what a mug! / by Lori Haskins Houran.
    p. cm. — (Little dogs rock!)
 Includes bibliographical references and index.
 ISBN-13: 978-1-59716-750-5 (library binding)
 ISBN-10: 1-59716-750-9 (library binding)
 1. Pug—Juvenile literature. I. Title.
 SF429.P9H37 2009
 636.76—dc22
                          2008040613

For more information, write to Bearport Publishing Company, Inc., 101 Fifth Avenue, Suite 6R, New York, New York 10003. Printed in the United States of America.

10 9 8 7 6 5 4 3 2 1

Contents

Dog on the Job

Isabella was crying. It was the little girl's fourth birthday, and she was in the hospital. All she wanted to do was go home.

The nurses tried to cheer her up. They brought her stuffed animals, funny cards, and balloons. Nothing made Isabella feel better . . . until Joseph the pug arrived.

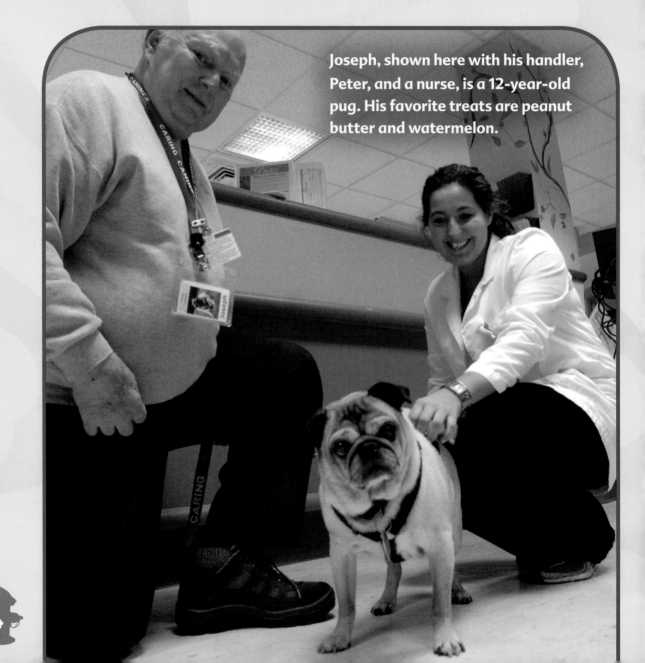

Joseph, shown here with his handler, Peter, and a nurse, is a 12-year-old pug. His favorite treats are peanut butter and watermelon.

Joseph's **handler**, Peter, plopped the small tan dog on the girl's bed. Right away, Joseph snuggled into Isabella's side. Isabella stopped sobbing.

Then Joseph laid his soft head on Isabella's belly. Isabella gave a shy smile.

Before long, Joseph was "kissing" Isabella all over her face. The little girl laughed out loud!

Pugs tend to be jolly dogs—even if they don't look it! Their wrinkled faces make them appear worried and cranky. For this reason, the Dutch name for pugs is *mopshond*, which means "grumbly dog."

▲ **Joseph cuddles with a friend at Winchester Hospital in Massachusetts.**

Lap of Luxury

Joseph is a **therapy dog**. He visits patients in hospitals and nursing homes. His job is to help these people feel better.

Making people happy comes naturally to pugs. In fact, it has always been their job. Pugs were first raised in China more than 2,000 years ago. They didn't pull sleds or herd sheep like other dogs. From the start, they were **companions**. Their job was to keep people company.

▼ Chinese emperors used to put pugs up their sleeves to keep themselves warm.

▲ A ceramic figure of a pug ancestor made almost 2,000 years ago

Pugs didn't "work" for just anyone. These small dogs sat in the laps of Chinese **monks**, emperors, and other important people. It was against the law for ordinary citizens to own pugs!

▲ Today's pugs still love lounging on people's laps.

How did pugs get their name? Some people think they were named after a small monkey, called a pug, which their faces resemble.

Crown Dogs

In the 1500s, European **traders** visited China. They were so impressed with the friendly little lap dogs they saw that they decided to take them home. Soon, pugs became a favorite among **royalty** in Europe, too. For example, Prince William, who lived in Holland during the 1500s, owned a pug named Pompey. One night, Pompey saved William's life by barking when the prince's enemies tried to sneak up on him. After that, pugs became the **official** dogs of the Dutch court.

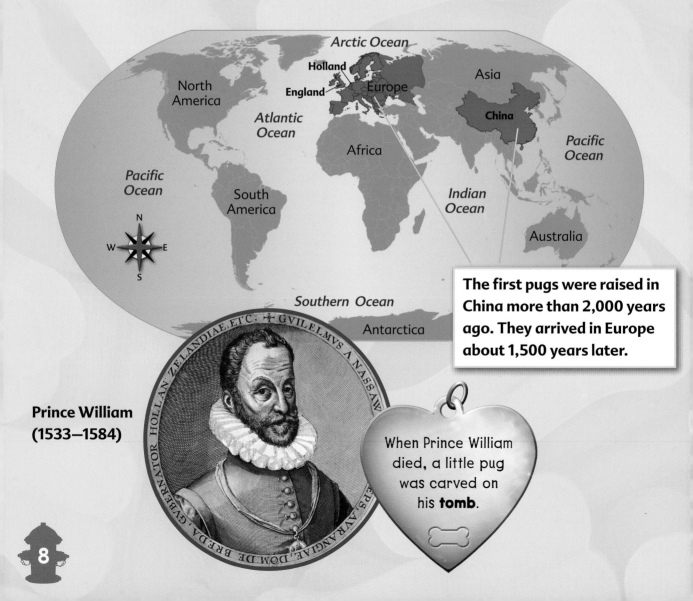

The first pugs were raised in China more than 2,000 years ago. They arrived in Europe about 1,500 years later.

Prince William (1533–1584)

When Prince William died, a little pug was carved on his **tomb**.

When William's great-grandson became the king of England in 1688, he took his favorite pugs along with him. Pugs stayed in the British royal family for hundreds of years. In the 1900s, the Duke and Duchess of Windsor kept more than ten pugs. Their pets even had their own servants, including a poop-picker-upper!

▲ The Duke and Duchess of Windsor, sitting with some of their pugs

Clowning Around

Today, many famous people still own pugs. Actresses Jessica Alba and Tori Spelling are big fans of the little dog. Jessica is often seen out and about with her two pugs, Sid and Nancy.

Tori Spelling with her pug, Mimi LaRue

▲ **Jessica Alba with her pugs, Sid and Nancy**

Actress Abigail Breslin is another pug lover. She told a reporter, "I want to get a pug, but my mom won't let me." Perhaps that's because Abigail already has a dog, two cats, and a tortoise!

It's no surprise that lots of people who are not famous enjoy having pugs as pets, too. These little dogs are known for being patient, loving, and playful. It seems as if they will do just about anything to entertain their owners— including getting dressed up in silly costumes! For this reason they are often called "the clowns of the dog world."

This pug is dressed up to look like the Energizer Bunny.

A pug dressed in a ▶
Superman costume

Funny Faces

Even without costumes, pugs are still funny. Just one look at the little dog's wrinkly face is enough to make anyone grin. Pugs also have big, googly eyes that always seem to be saying something—usually "Feed me!" or "Pet me!"

▲ Since a pug's eyes stick out, they can easily be injured. They can even pop out of their sockets.

Pugs are noisy dogs, too. They make all sorts of sounds. Why? Their noses are pushed in, which can make it hard for them to breathe. So they often snort, snore, sneeze, and wheeze. Pugs make another noise, too—they fart!

Pugs are at risk for many health problems, including trouble with their teeth and hips. A **veterinarian** can help treat many of these problems.

▲ It's important for pug owners to take their pets to a veterinarian regularly.

Little Dogs, Big Muscles

Pugs stand only about one foot (12 in) tall and weigh around 15 pounds (7 kg). Yet these funny, noisy dogs are sturdy, with a surprising amount of muscle. It's often said that pugs are big dogs in small bodies!

A pug's body is as strong as the body of a larger dog.

Pugs have tightly curled tails and soft, short coats. Some have "double coats," which means they have one coat on top of the other. Most pugs are tan, also called fawn, or black. There are silver pugs, too, although they are very rare. All pugs, even fawn and silver ones, have black ears and a black **muzzle**.

Rose ears

Pugs' ears are soft and velvety and come in two different shapes. "Rose" ears fold forward, showing the insides of the ears. "Button" ears also fold forward, but they lie close to the head.

▲ **Button ears**

Tender Loving Care

Taking care of a pug is not hard work, but it requires a lot of time. Pug owners must **groom** their dogs in many ways. They need to wash their pets' faces often so dirt doesn't build up in the wrinkles. They have to brush their pugs' coats once a week and trim their nails every other week. Owners also need to take their pugs for daily walks—even if their pets **resist**! It's easy for these dogs to become overweight, since they love to eat and they don't love to exercise.

Some people think that because pugs have short coats, they don't shed much. That's not true! Pugs shed a lot. Washing and brushing their coats can help, but pug owners still need good vacuum cleaners!

When it's cold, pugs should go only on short walks, and they should wear a sweater to keep warm. They should not be taken for walks in very hot weather.

The most important part of caring for a pug is giving it attention. Pugs are very **social**. They need to be around people to be happy. "They're **Velcro** dogs," says Bill, a pug owner in Maine. "They stick right to your side!"

Pugs like to go everywhere with their owners, even kayaking.

Who, Me?

Since pugs love to please people, it seems as though they should be easy to train. However, that's not the case. Why? Pugs are stubborn. It's hard to convince them to change their ways.

An owner trying to train his pug to "stay."

New owners often get frustrated when their puppies chew up their shoes or go to the bathroom inside the house . . . over and over again. Sometimes people even give up on their pugs. Luckily, pug rescue organizations take in dogs that have been **abandoned**. Joseph was once in pug rescue. His first owners thought he couldn't learn to **obey**—and now he's a trained therapy dog! "It takes time to get through to a pug," says Peter, Joseph's handler. "Time, and lots of treats!"

◀ **This rescued pug is on its way to a new, loving home.**

Some pugs are abandoned because they are sick or old. Sophie, an older pug, was left out on the street one winter. Luckily, she was saved by Pug Rescue of Central New York, which found her a loving home.

Pug Pups

Pugs are little from the very start. When they're born, they're only about the size of a mouse. Mother pugs usually have small **litters**—around two to five pups. In the beginning, the newborns' eyes are closed. They can't do much of anything except drink their mother's milk.

A typical newborn pug weighs around seven ounces (1 kg).

Pugs are born with straight tails! Their tails don't start to curl until they're a few days old.

At about ten days old, the pugs' eyes open up, and they start trying to crawl. By six weeks, the puppies are walking, barking, and playing.

Pugs stay with their mothers until they are about three months old. Then most pups are adopted by families and become pets. A few, though, learn to **compete** in dog shows.

Pug puppies at play

Almost Perfect

To compete in a dog show, a pug has to look a certain way. It has to match a description, or **standard**, set by the **American Kennel Club**. Is its head large and round? Is its coat soft and smooth? Are its eyes bold and lively? There is no perfect dog, but the pug that comes as close as possible to the standard will win.

A pug being presented during a dog show

At dog shows, pugs first compete with other pugs. The dog that wins goes on to the Best in Group competition. Pugs are part of the **toy** group, which also includes other small **breeds** such as terriers and poodles. Finally, the top dogs from each group compete for the biggest prize—**Best in Show.**

▲ **Dogs from the toy group compete at a dog show.**

In terms of size, the pug is the biggest breed in the toy group. The smallest is the Chihuahua (chu-WHA-wha).

Top Dogs

The pug with the most wins in dog show history is named Dermot. Before this fawn-colored pug **retired**, he earned 65 Best in Show titles!

▲ In 2005, Dermot and his handler, Barry Clothier, traveled more than 55,000 miles (88, 514 km) so the pug could compete in dog shows around the country.

However, there was one show that Dermot did *not* win—the Westminster Kennel Club Dog Show. This is the biggest dog show in America. In its 132 years, only one pug has ever won Best in Show—three-year-old Chucky. He took the top prize in 1981. Sadly, Chucky died during an airplane trip the very next year. He was returning home from another competition, where he had once again won Best in Show.

Show dogs have two names. Their "call name" is the name they use every day. Their "registered name" is a fancy name that's used when they compete in dog shows. Chucky's registered name was Ch. Dhandy's Favorite Woodchuck. The "Ch." at the beginning of a dog's name means that it's a champion.

◀ **Chucky, winning Best in Show at the Westminster Dog Show**

Can't Get Enough

Most pugs are pets, not champion show dogs. Yet their owners still think they're superstars! Pug owners are known for being **passionate** about their dogs. Some fill their homes with pug statues, pug clocks, and pug paintings. Others fill their homes with . . . more pugs!

Debbie lives in New York. She started off with one pug. Then she got another. Now she's up to four. "I can't help it," says Debbie. "They're so lovable!"

Debbie's pugs—Rocco (top), TJ (left), Margarita (center), and Harley (right)

Of course, pugs are not for everyone. Even Debbie agrees. "They need a lot of care," she cautions, "and they have minds of their own." For the right kind of owner, though, pugs can be wonderful, funny friends.

▲ **Debbie and her husband with their beloved pugs**

Some pug owners join pug clubs to share their love of the little dogs. The Pug Club of America was founded in 1931. Today, there are groups in nearly every state in the country and in many nations around the world, including Finland and Australia.

Pugs at a Glance

Weight:	14–18 pounds (6–8 kg)
Height at Shoulder:	12–15 inches (30–38 cm)
Coat Hair:	Short; some have a "double coat"
Colors:	Fawn or black; silver, though rarely
Country of Origin:	China
Life Span:	About 15 years
Personality:	Playful, patient, loving

Best in Show

What makes a great pug? Every owner knows that his or her dog is special. Judges in dog shows, however, look very carefully at a pug's appearance and behavior. Here are some of the things they look for:

dark, bold, lively eyes

large, round head

velvety ears; can be "rose" or "button"

tightly curled tail, preferably with two curls

deep wrinkles and short muzzle

soft, smooth coat

square and muscular body

Behavior:
playful, charming, and outgoing

Glossary

abandoned (uh-BAN-duhnd) left alone, without help

American Kennel Club (uh-MER-uh-kuhn KEN-uhl KLUHB) a national organization that is involved in many activities having to do with dogs, including setting rules for dog shows

Best in Show (BEST IN SHOH) the top-rated dog in a dog show

breeds (BREEDZ) types of dogs

companions (kuhm-PAN-yuhnz) animals or people who spend time with someone

compete (kuhm-PEET) to try to do better than someone else in a contest

groom (GROOM) to keep an animal neat and clean

handler (HAND-lur) someone who trains and works with animals

litters (LIT-urz) groups of animals, such as puppies or kittens, that are born to the same mother at the same time

monks (MUHNGKS) men who live in special religious communities

muzzle (MUHZ-uhl) a dog's nose, mouth, and jaw area

obey (oh-BAY) to follow orders

official (uh-FISH-uhl) when something has been approved by a person in charge

passionate (PASH-uh-nit) showing very strong feelings

resist (ri-ZIST) to refuse to do something

retired (ri-TYE-urd) no longer working, usually due to age

royalty (ROY-uhl-tee) kings, queens, princes, and princesses

social (SOH-shuhl) enjoy the company of others

standard (STAN-durd) the description of the "perfect" dog in each breed

therapy dog (THER-uh-pee DAWG) a dog that visits hospitals and other places to cheer up people and make them feel more comfortable

tomb (TOOM) a place where someone is buried

toy (TOY) tiny, when related to dogs

traders (TRAY-derz) people who buy, sell, or trade goods

Velcro (VEL-kroh) a fastener that consists of two pieces of fabric; one piece is covered with tiny hooks that stick to tiny loops on the second piece of fabric

veterinarian (*vet*-ur-uh-NER-ee-uhn) a doctor who cares for animals

Bibliography

Belmote, Brenda. *The Pug Handbook.* Hauppauge, NY: Barron's (2004).

Bourgeois, Dianne. *Pugs.* Neptune City, NJ: TFH Publications, Inc. (2006).

Thornton, Kim Campbell. *The Everything Pug Book.* Avon, MA: Adams Media (2005).

Read More

Gray, Susan H. *Pugs (Domestic Dogs).* Chanhassen, MN: Child's World (2007).

Rake, Jody S. *Pugs.* Mankato, MN: Capstone Press (2006).

Stone, Lynn M. *Pugs (Eye to Eye with Dogs).* Vero Beach, FL: Rourke Publishing (2007).

Learn More Online

To learn more about pugs, visit
www.bearportpublishing.com/LittleDogsRock

Index

About the Author

Lori Haskins Houran has been writing and editing children's books since 1992.
She lives in New York City with her two sons.